Supporting Families Through Their Grief, Loss & Change

DAPHNE VALCOURT,
PhD, CPsyD, LMFT, LMHC, CQSW

*   *   *   *   *

To order additional copies of this book, contact:
Xlibris
844-714-8691
www.Xlibris.com
Orders@Xlibris.com

ISBN: Softcover   979-8-3694-3163-4
         EBook   979-8-3694-3209-9

Print information available on the last page

Rev. date: 10/23/2024

Supporting Families Through Their Grief, Loss & Change

Table of Contents

Introduction

- This little book is entitled **Supporting Individuals & Families Through *Their Grief, Loss & Change*** because the purpose of this book is to help individuals and families process their grief, accept their loss, make positive changes and move forward with their lives rather than stay stuck in the clutches of their grief and pain.

- The idea for this book emerged after losing several family members within a two - year span during the Corona Virus pandemic of 2019 (otherwise referred to as COVID-19) and feeling the need to provide support while being supported. I also saw that there were those who were stuck in their grief and needed help to make changes and move on with their lives.

- My appreciation goes out to my immediate family, and my church family with whom I have shared this information and was encouraged by them to share this information with a wider audience. Special appreciation goes out to Pastor Stafford Byers who first gave me the opportunity to share this information with his congregation and to Loni Adeniran for checking for errors in this book. This book is intended for educational purposes only; you are encouraged to seek out the services of a grief counselor to help you work through your grief and loss.

Grief & Loss

One of the realities of life is the experience of grief and loss. At some point or another, we will all experience grief and loss. What is Grief? Grief is the emotional response to loss. It is a paradoxical emotional response caught between hope and despair. In the case of a loss due to death, there is hope for those who believe in a resurrection and yet there is despair over losing the loved one.

Grief is not considered a negative emotion; rather, it is an emotion that is associated with pain and loss - especially if the loss is traumatic. Grief is also associated with love – a bond of affection that is disrupted.

The term bereavement is often used interchangeably with grief but the two are not one and the same. Bereavement is the state of loss, while grief is the reaction to loss - particularly to the loss of someone or some thing to which a bond or affection was formed. If we love a lot, we will grieve a lot because grief is the reaction to that loss. The deeper the love, the deeper the pain and the longer the grief process

Grief and the Brain

Mary-Frances O'Connor is a psychologist who studied neuroimaging of grief and the brain. She found that when a relationship is formed, a bond is created and the memory is encoded in the brain. When we bond with a loved one, the encoding of that relationship in the brain comes along with an everlasting belief—the belief that they will be there for us, and we will be there for them. Losing a loved one therefore not only disrupts one's life but their absence also disrupts the brain functioning and neurotransmitters. It's as though you have lost a part of yourself. In her book _The Grieving Brain_, published in 2022, O'Connor explains how understanding this insight can help us to better understand bereavement and have self-compassion. "Grief is the cost of loving someone," she writes. When our loved one dies, that moment becomes a  memory. It could be the memory of watching them decline and being with them at the bedside, or a memory of that terrible phone call that bore news of their death. Memories are but one kind of information that the brain relies on.

Things we grieve over

There are many things we can lose and grieve over. Death is not the only thing we grieve over. The following are some examples:

- Loss of loved ones as in the case of Lazarus where Jesus wept over his passing.
- Losing a child as with Mary, the mother of Jesus. She wept when her son was crucified and was seen weeping outside of Jesus' tomb
- Loss of innocence as in Tamar's case – she was deceived and raped by her brother
- Loss of health or a negative medical diagnosis as in Hezekiah's case who was sick unto death
- Aging and loss of youth, and feeling cast aside as in David's case – (Psalm 71:9)
- Loss of self concept, identity or how you define yourself as in Saul's case when he was replaced as King by David and the people lauded David instead of him.
- Disappointed hopes & dreams (not how things should be) as with the Children of Israel by the Rivers of Babylon (Ps. 137),
- Naomi who lost her family while migrants in a foreign land.
- Loss of Role or Status – unexpected life changes as with Joseph who was sold into slavery and imprisoned and Hannah who was childless and desired motherhood.
- Loss of sense of self through addictions as with Solomon and his many wives.
- Loss of relationships – loss of spouse, friend, loss of a child by a parent – Jacob and Job experienced a series of losses in their relationships and in their lives.

Children & Grief

- Children's response to grief is often determined by the response of those around them. Children may cry because they observe adults around them crying or because of anxiety over the separation, but Infants and toddlers have no concept of death. Children's level of maturity of thought and ability to conceptualize will determine how they process their feelings. Teenagers know that death is permanent and may react to the loss based on cultural beliefs, their family's response or their understanding about death and loss.

Quote on Grief From Kluber-Ross

- *This grief, shame, and guilt are not very far removed from feelings of anger and rage. The process of grief always includes some qualities of anger. Since none of us likes to admit anger at a deceased person, these emotions are often disguised or repressed and prolong the period of grief or show up in other ways. It is well to remember that it is not up to us to judge such feelings as bad or shameful but to understand their true meaning and origin as something very human. In order to illustrate this, I will again use the example of the child -- and the child in us. The five-year-old who loses his mother is both blaming himself for her disappearance and being angry at her for having deserted him and for no longer gratifying his needs. The dead person then*  *turns into something the child loves and wants very much but also hates with equal intensity for this severe deprivation. Excerpted from Death & Dying by Elizabeth Kluber-Ross*

Grief Triggers

- Holidays and birthdays, can be an especially difficult time for those who have lost loved ones because these events trigger memories of the loved one. Maybe this person played a critical role in making the holidays special and now that person is not there. Secrets revealed after the loss can be especially painful because the secrets were never told or resolved.

- These memories can lead to what we call "grief triggers". It can reawaken painful memories and feelings of the loss that has happened. At times, these feelings can just pop up and catch you off guard – you might experience periods of sadness and depression, and you might even spend time questioning your response. The

"what ifs" questions or the maybe "I should have" thoughts may also surface. You might even be wondering if there is anything you could have done differently to prevent the loss. This is not unusual. It is important to put a name to what you are feeling – that name is called *grief*. Indeed, the more bonds of affection we form, the more grief we will experience. By giving the emotion a name, you can begin to heal. You cannot heal what you cannot name. Once you give the emotion a name, you can begin to free yourself by talking about it.

Types of Grief

- People go through different types of grief. **There is anticipatory grief, normal grief and complicated grief.** Our reactions to grief can affect us physically, psychologically, or cognitively.

- **Anticipatory grief** occurs when the loss is expected as with terminal illness. Because the loss is expected, there is time for preparation, and opportunity to settle unresolved conflicts. In addition, the grief response may not seem normal to some because having begun the grief process sometimes months or years earlier than others, they may not show open grief at the passing of the individual.

- **Normal grief** is the usual feeling of grief that might occur days and weeks after the loss. The grief reaction might be crying spells, sleep problems, lack of energy, difficulty concentrating, feelings of anger, guilt, loneliness etc.

Complicated Grief

- Complicated grief can take on different forms and include:

- *Chronic* or Prolonged grief, which is similar to normal grief but extends over a longer period - many years. Anniversaries and holidays are often grief triggers that bring back memories of the loss.

- *Delayed grief* is suppressed or postponed feelings to avoid dealing with the loss.

- *Masked grief is pretending that all is well; saying* I am fine, but the behavioral symptoms say something else. Such displaced feelings may also involve drinking or drugging, sexual acting out behavior –having multiple indiscriminate sex partners.

- *Disenfranchised grief* is being in an illicit or socially unacceptable relationship that ends, such as an affair, rape or an abortion, but you cannot share it with anyone because it was not a relationship or behavior that was socially sanctioned.

- *Betrayal grief* occurs when a family, spouse or friend abandons you or cheats on you resulting in a betrayal of trust and a feeling of being "stabbed in the back" by the betrayer. Jesus experienced betrayal grief from Peter and Judas. Judas sold him out and Peter denied ever knowing him (Matthew 26:14-16, Luke 22:55-62).

Disenfranchised grief

- Disenfranchised grief is associated with shame or a socially unacceptable loss. It is loss that the mourner may have difficulty talking about because of its hidden nature. Such losses may include an aborted pregnancy, death by suicide, or AIDS; or even the death of someone with whom the mourner was having a secret affair. These losses carry a stigma, for which society does not share a sympathetic view, so the mourner is denied the opportunity to grieve openly or receive communal support.

Prolonged Grief

- Prolonged grief may often follow the loss experienced and is most often connected to how the loss or death occurred. If the loss was sudden, accidental, violent, malicious or if there was no preparation, such as in the death of a child or death in a hospital intensive care unit, as during COVID and there was no opportunity to say goodbye, or maybe there was no expectation that the person would die; this could prolong the grief process. If the relationship with the person was very close and now you must go on in life without that person, the loss can derail you. Prolonged grief can sap the very life out of you. You can be physically alive but spiritually dead on the inside. Prolonged grief can do great harm to your health because it tends to dry up the marrow. Prov 17:22 says a broken spirit dries up the bones. If you feel your bones are dry from prolonged grief you may wonder, "can these dry bones live again?" Well, I am here to tell you that based on the assurances of Ezekiel 37, "yes, these dry bones can live again." Verse 5 says: *Thus, saith the Lord God unto these bones; Behold, I will cause breath to enter into you, and ye shall live (Ez. 37:5).*

Biblical Examples of Grief

- The Bible provides several examples of grief and loss.

- Genesis 6:6 says that God grieves because of man's sin. Sin and iniquities have separated man from God. God was grieved at his heart over the loss of his face-to-face contact, with mankind. He also grieved at the hardness of men's hearts. The Lord was sorry that He had made man on the earth, and it grieved his heart. It's like a parent who grieves over their children when the parent sees them heading in the wrong direction or making poor choices. This is can be heartbreaking for the parent

- In Gen 23:2, Sarah and Abraham were living apart. Sarah was in Hebron, and Abraham was in Beersheba. Sarah died in Hebron, Abraham mourned for Sarah and went to Hebron to bury her. This was the first burial or funeral in the bible and first record of someone crying. Abraham also grieved for his son Ishmael when he was forced to send him away because he was very attached to Ishmael. We see the two brothers Isaac & Ishmael reuniting at their father Abraham's funeral. Funerals help with the grief process. It reunites families, and provides support in coping with the loss, which helps with the grief process.

Biblical Examples of Grief

Naomi was a foreigner in Moab. She and her family went to Moab for a better life but while in Moab she lost her husband and her two sons. The losses didn't happen in a day. It was a build up of years of disappointments and losses. She suffered layers of grief and set back (Ruth 1: 20-21). Naomi in her depression blamed God for her losses. She said the Lord has dealt bitterly with me. She felt abandoned by God but in Naomi's story even in her grief and loss God had not abandoned her. She found support in her friendship with her daughter-in-law Ruth. When we lose a loved one, we do not know how things will end up, but as in Naomi's case we can trust and believe that God has a plan. Ruth married Boaz and through that union came kings —even the king of kings – Jesus our Savior.

- **Joseph was Jacob's beloved son who was sold into slavery, but his brothers led their father to believe that he was killed by a wild animal.** Gen 37:34-36 says that **Jacob mourned for Joseph a long time. Losing a child is not the norm. Parents do not expect their children to precede them in death.** In Joseph's case Jacob refused to be comforted and said "I will go to my grave mourning for my son," so Jacob kept grieving.

- **In 2 Samuel 13, Tamar, daughter of David and sister to Absalom was raped by her half-brother Amnon resulting in the loss of innocence.** She tore her robe, put ashes on her head, wept and remained a desolate woman in her brother's house - she went into a state of depression.

Biblical Examples of Grief

- **Jesus wept at the loss of his friend Lazarus** (John 11:35). In some societies men are socialized not to cry but here Jesus wept over the loss of his friend. Tears are a good way of releasing stress and emotional pain. Crying is a safety valve. It's interesting that the Bible records major biblical figures – men – Jesus, David, and Abraham crying over experiencing the loss of loved ones, so it's not true that "real men don't cry." These biblical examples are real men who were certainly connected to their emotions.

- **Ezekiel the prophet was told by God that his dear wife -** his beloved wife – the desire of his eyes - the woman he loved was about to die suddenly, but as an object lesson, God tells him that he is not to mourn in the customary way - wearing sackcloth and ashes. Instead, he should just groan to himself **(Ez. 24:15-18)**. The directive from God seems an odd one but it required an act of faith that even in our grief we can trust God and have a steadfast faith in him.

- **The widow of Nain lost her only son**. When Jesus saw the funeral procession, his heart was overflowed with compassion. "Don't cry!" he said. Then he walked over to the coffin and touched it, and the bearers stopped. "Young man," he said, "I tell you, get up." Then the dead boy sat up and began to talk! And Jesus gave him back to his mother (Luke 7:11-15 NLT).

Benefits of crying

Crying serves as a natural response to strong emotional pain or sometimes even pleasure. Crying is said to occur as a result of the sympathetic nervous system being activated in response to your emotions. In grief, crying helps to ease emotional pain by releasing oxytocin or endorphins which are considered the feel good chemicals. According to researchers, emotional tears are said to flush stress hormones and other toxins out of our system, so it is important to allow yourself to cry if you feel like it.

Stages of Grief

- Elizabeth Kubler-Ross, a Swiss Psychiatrist was the first to study the stages of grief published in her 1969 book *Death and Dying.* The stages are identified as *shock or denial, anger, bargaining, depression, and acceptance.* David Kessler, a grief expert later identified a sixth stage called *Finding meaning* –a stage that transforms grief into a more peaceful and hopeful experience.

- Denial – In a state of denial, you may experience a feeling of numbness. You may also try to find an alternate explanation – it cannot be true.

- Anger –During anger you may experience a loss of control and feeling like a failure. You may ask why me? You may tell yourself "I Should-a" or "could-a " done some things differently. You may even express anger at God for taking your loved one.

- Bargaining – In the bargaining state you may tell yourself that if I go to church, maybe God will bring the person back or God will change things.

- Depression – is that state of feeling helpless, or hopeless; it is at this point you may realize you cannot change the situation.

- Acceptance – Finally there is acceptance that the loss has occurred – that a chapter has ended and another beginning.

- The patriarch Job suffered multiple losses and went through all the stages of grief here identified.

STAGES OF GRIEF

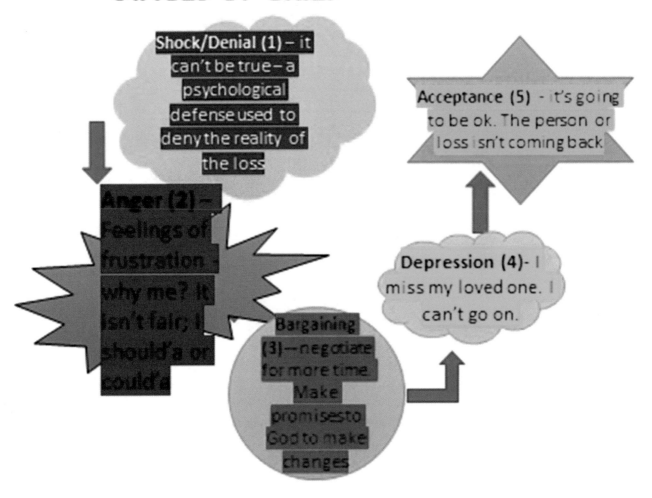

Shock/Denial (1) – it can't be true – a psychological defense used to deny the reality of the loss

Anger (2) – Feelings of frustration – why me? It isn't fair; I should'a or could'a

Bargaining (3) – negotiate for more time. Make promises to God to make changes

Depression (4) – I miss my loved one. I can't go on.

Acceptance (5) – it's going to be ok. The person or loss isn't coming back

Job and his grief process

- The patriarch Job is an example of someone who experienced grief over the loss of his estate, his children and his health. In his grief, we see him going through the grief process. First, we see him in grief over losing his property and his children; he rented his mantle; shaved his head and falling upon the ground, he worshipped but seems to bounce back quickly - seemingly because of his philosophy of life and his relationship with God. We see him acknowledging God as the giver of all that he possessed. He said – *Naked I came from my mother's womb and naked I will depart .. the Lord gave and the Lord hath taken away; blessed be the name of the Lord.* When he lost his health however, we see Job in

prolonged grief. In anger at his suffering, his wife questioned his faithfulness and told him he might as well curse God and die; but again, Job's view of life is that we receive both good and evil at the hand of God; he felt that God had turned away from him. In Job's anger he cursed the day that he was born (not God). In the bargaining phase of grief – he said "I would speak to the almighty and I desire to argue my case with God. How many are my iniquities and my sins? Make me to know my transgression and my sin;" In his depression – feeling helpless and hopeless, he said -I will speak in the anguish of my spirit; I will complain in the bitterness of my soul. In his depression, he said: *"Oh that my grief were thoroughly weighed, and my calamity laid in the balances together."*

Job expresses his feelings

- Job gives voice to his suffering by questioning the purpose of living and complaining in the bitterness of his soul. He mentioned having scary dreams and night terrors which is not an uncommon grief response; and finally, acceptance. Job acknowledges his limited understanding of the events of his life and concludes by seeing God in a different way – as all powerful and all knowing. We don't know how long Job suffered in his grief but what we do know is that Job did not give up on God.

- As in Job's case, it is important to acknowledge your feelings and put a name to what you are feeling; identify that you are experiencing grief. Reflect on what the loss of the person or the position meant to you, talk about your grief and acknowledge that the person or position is gone. Acknowledge your feelings of sadness and communicate your feelings.

- Job expresses forgiveness of those who did him wrong and receives countless blessings and restoration.

Prolonged grief as a mental disorder

- The Diagnostic and Statistical Manual of Mental Disorder (DSM) 5 has listed prolonged grief as a mental disorder because it is possible to get stuck in any of these phases of grief. Getting stuck in your grief may leave you feeling like a part of you has died, you might experience disbelief about the loss, avoidance of reminders that the person is gone, intense anger, bitterness or sorrow related to the loss - and difficulty re-engaging in life.

Factors that can impact how you grieve

- Closeness to the situation or person (physical proximity to the person) will impact how you grieve. The loss of a child as in Jacob's case can leave the feeling of a hole in the heart because it is not the natural or expected order of things. A child is not expected to die before a parent.

- The number of stressors in your life at the time of the loss can exacerbate the grief process.

- How much control you had in the situation related to the loss, or the relationship with the individual may leave you feeling depressed or hopeless because you do not know how to go on

or you worry that no one is coming to help or rescue you. An example of this is that of Tamar who had not anticipated a rape, nor did she have control over her brother or his actions. As a result, she felt hopeless and helpless and went into depression.

Factors that can impact how you grieve

- Mental health issues – if you were experiencing depression and anxiety before the loss, the most recent loss may add another layer to the losses already experienced and was not processed previously and may put you into deeper depression.

- Your coping skills – your resilience; religious beliefs/ routine, faith may serve to strengthen you. Job's belief that ownership belongs to God, helped him cope with the loss of his children and his assets. He resolved that the Lord gave him what he had, and the Lord has taken it away.

- Having social supports – may include biological family, friends, church family

- Your understanding of loss and its meaning to you – How you cognitively understand and interpret the loss matters. Do you see it as the end of life altogether or the possibility of a new beginning? Do you believe in a resurrection and that you will see your loved one again?

- Blame- Do you blame self, God, others or the situation? Martha blamed Jesus when her brother Lazarus died. She said: "If you had been here my brother would not have died."

- Denial – You may go into denial to numb the pain or to protect yourself

- You may express anger at yourself, God, others -You may ask "Why did this happen?" Your response will rest on your philosophy of life and death

Responding to Grief

Common grief reactions include:

- Shock, disbelief, or denial and can last for days or months. You may be angry at God or the deceased or the loss experienced.

- You may experience periods of sadness or depression – frequent crying, headaches; isolation. Loss of sleep and loss of appetite; distress – feeling like there is a hole in the heart

- Bargaining with God and making promises about changes you will make

- Acceptance – Reflection on what the person meant to you.

- Acknowledging that the person is gone

- Identifying that you are experiencing grief is often the first step towards healing.

- Acknowledge and Communicate your feelings; pray, exercise, do art or music; go to church, or join a grief recovery support group.

Things to Remember when grieving

❖ Some people who have lost loved ones may go to seances and seek to make contact with the dead, but the Bible warns against doing so. It says: Do not turn to mediums or seek out spirits, for you will be defiled by them. I am the LORD your God.' (Leviticus 19:31, <u>NIV</u>).

❖ Things to Remember: There are many faces of grief & no two people grieve the same way. People go through the phases of grief - *Denial, Anger, Bargaining and Depression, Acceptance* – differently. Some people may stay in one phase of grief longer than others due to their loss experience and mitigating factors.

❖ Ambiguous loss, as during COVID where the loss occurs without closure or clear understanding can complicate and delay the process of grieving.

❖ Anxiety and depression could be related to layers of unresolved grief and loss. Multiple deaths of close relatives, divorce and other life changes can compound the grief process and lead to depression and anxiety.

How grief impacts your spirit

- Grief may have you feeling like you have a hole in your heart.

- Grief breaks your spirit. Prov 17:22 says a joyful heart is good medicine but a broken spirit dries up the bones. The opposite of a joyful heart is a crushed spirit –grief. Grief can sit in your spirit like dry bones, but Ez. 37:1-14 says God led Ezekiel to a valley of dry bones and brings life to the bones – so all hope is not lost. Is 61: 2-3 reminds us that Jesus was sent to comfort all those who mourn and provide for those who grieve… to give them beauty instead of ashes, the oil of joy instead of mourning and a garment of praise instead of despair.

- As Christians we grieve with hope. Hebrews 4:15-16 says:

- [15] For we have not an high priest which cannot be touched with the feeling of our infirmities; but was in all points tempted like as we are, yet without sin. Jesus understands our grief. A Song by the Heritage Singers says: God sees the tears of a broken - hearted soul; he sees our tears even when they fall. God weeps along with man and takes him by the hand; tears are a language God understands.

- [16] Let us therefore come boldly unto the throne of grace, that we may obtain mercy, and find grace to help in time of need.

- Draw close to *"the Father of mercies and God of all comfort, who comforts us in all our affliction"* (2 Corinthians 1:3–4, ESV).

Ego focused Emotions

- Unforgiveness, anger and fear are three ego-focused emotions that can result from the loss or hurt experienced. Ego focused emotions are those emotions that are focused on yourself, your wishes, needs and desires and you make your feelings your central focus. It is important to surrender those feelings in order to grow. Pray for a willingness to see things differently. The opposite of fear is faith, so open your heart to God and ask him to restore your faith in him if the anger is directed at God. If the loss or hurt resulted from malicious means, choose to forgive the one who has done you wrong. In doing so, you are releasing the control and power that the offender had over your life. Ultimately this will help to free you of the hurt you are feeling. The Lord's prayer is a reminder of the importance of forgiving those who have done you wrong.

- *Proverbs 29:11 says: A fool gives full vent to their anger but the wise quietly holds it back (NKJV)*

Forgiveness Statement

- If you are harboring anger, begin by releasing harbored anger with prayer. When negative emotions arise, write a statement of forgiveness.

- Begin by telling yourself that I am human and I am hurt.

- Tell yourself that I now choose to let go of my hurt and forgive myself first for holding on to my hurt.

- If someone did you wrong, state, I choose to forgive (write the name of whoever caused you hurt)

- State what happened and the hardest thing to forgive.

- Write what it is that you are letting go of.

- State what you will do moving forward to continue letting go.

- If your body tenses, stop and take deep breaths; breathe from the abdomen. Pretend you are smelling a rose and blowing out a candle to help you practice deep breathing.

Memorialize the loss

- Just because the loss has occurred doesn't mean memories of the loss or the person will disappear; nor does the memory have to end in despair or sadness.

- Memorialize the Loss by extending yourself to engage in acts of service.

- It is possible to create a meaningful memorial such as planting a pine tree or a rosebush if the person was cremated or marking the burial spot with a headstone.

- Make a memorial quilt with articles of clothing of the loved one

- Establish a grant or a scholarship fund, donate to a worthy cause or simply live the life the deceased would have wanted for you

- Write about the loss and how the experience has impacted you.

- Create a memory book or video of time spent together.

Grief Reminders

- ❖ Grief is a process you will have to go through

- ❖ No one can tell you how to feel or when to stop grieving

- ❖ From time to time, you will experience mixed emotions especially when triggered by a reminder of the loss

- ❖ Others may make judgmental remarks and tell you not to be angry –especially at God

- ❖ God understands your feelings even when you question his love and care

- ❖ Be around people who will allow you to grieve and are comfortable with your tears

- ❖ Unhelpful words of comfort such as "it's God's will" or "he is in a better place," are well meaning and are said to comfort you but may not help to soothe your pain.

- ❖ Treasure your memories and share them with others

- ❖ Rely on your faith to see you through and express it in ways that seem appropriate to you

- ❖ Be patient with yourself. The death of a loved one results in changes in your life that will require adjustments.

Action Plan

- Action Plan: It is important to face the loss; talk about it and give the feelings a name. That name is called – grief. Remove any walls that stop you from talking about your loss. Address feelings of hopelessness and helplessness by focusing on what can be changed versus what cannot be changed. Redefine your view of the situation and visualize a positive future

- Steps towards healing

- Acknowledge that grief may take a year or two to heal. Journal your thoughts and feelings in the process.

- Be aware of grief triggers – memories; holidays, smells, songs, or clothing

- Take care of yourself; get plenty of rest, eat a balanced diet, stay away from drugs & alcohol and follow a normal routine

- The loss may not make any sense but Joseph's story in Gen. 37 & 38 is a reminder that grief and loss can work together for good - even though the loss may not make any sense. Naomi grieved the loss of her sons and her husband but was able to see Ruth marry Boaz - through whose lineage came king David, and finally Jesus – king of kings.

Making the Change

- After a loss of any kind, it can leave you feeling lost and directionless so it is important to reassess your situation and redefine yourself. Ask yourself these questions:

- Who am I without this person in my life, this job, or this relationship?

- What do I want my life to look like moving forward?

- What goals do I need to accomplish moving forward?

- What one behavior do I need to change in order to move forward?

- What one negative belief have I held about myself that I need to change in order to grow?

Scriptures of comfort during grief

He heals the brokenhearted and binds up their wounds. – **Psalm 147:3 (NIV)**

The Lord is close to the brokenhearted and saves those who are crushed in spirit. – **Psalm 34:18 (NIV)**

Weeping may stay for the night, but rejoicing comes in the morning. – **Psalm 30:5 (NIV)**

My flesh and my heart may fail, but God is the strength of my heart and my portion forever. – **Psalm 73:26 (NIV)**

Blessed are those who mourn, for they will be comforted. – **Matthew 5:4**

For no one is cast off by the Lord forever. Though He brings grief, He will show compassion. So great is His unfailing love. For He does not willingly bring affliction or grief to anyone. – **Lamentations 3:31-33 (NIV)**

…God himself will be with them and be their God. He will wipe every tear from their eyes. There will be no more death or mourning or crying or pain, for the old order of things has passed away…. [He is making everything new]–Revelation 21:3-5 (NIV)

Notes/Action Plan/Goals

Redefine yourself and write your goals here. Be specific and provide anticipated completion dates for your goals to be accomplished:

1. _____

_____

_____

2. _____

_____

_____

3. _____

_____

_____

4. _____

_____

_____

Source
Materials

- Bibles used include King James Version (1972) & New King James Version (1982) Thomas Nelson Pub. New International Version (2011) Biblica Pub.

- Newhouse, L. (2021) Is crying good for you. Harvard Health,

- Houben, L. (2017) Transforming Grief & Loss Workbook. PESI Pub.

- Klass, D., Silverman, P. R., & Nickman, S. L. (Eds.). (1996). *Continuing bonds: New understandings of grief.* Taylor & Francis.

- Kubler-Ross, E (1969) On death & dying

- Kübler-Ross, E. Kessler, D. (2014) On Grief and Grieving: Finding the Meaning of Grief Through the Five Stages of Loss.

- O'Connor, M. (2022) The Grieving Brain: The Surprising Science of How We Learn from Love and Loss – February 1, 2022

  https://maryfrancesoconner.org/book

- White, E. G. (2024) Mind Character & Personality. egwritings.org

- Worden, W.J. (2018) Counseling and Grief therapy (5th ed). Springer Pub.

About the Author

When it comes to understanding the emotional turmoil of grief, loss and change, Dr Valcourt certainly understands because she has experienced it all. Dr Valcourt was born in Jamaica, West Indies and raised by her grandmother. Upon returning from school at age 11, she found her grandmother in bed complaining of feeling unwell, which was most unusual because her grandmother was only 62 years old and always very active. Within three hours of returning from school, while sitting on the bed next to her grandmother, the unexpected happened. Her grandmother had a massive heart attack and passed away. This was a traumatic experience for a child. Her grandmother's death resulted in her joining her parents in London, England. Leaving the warmth of sunny Jamaica to the chilly shores of London was another loss and major change and adjustment. In London she attended Secondary School and Universities where she obtained professional qualifications in teaching and social work and a Master's degree in Sociology and Social Policy. Having a desire to further understand human behavior, she left London and went to Loma Linda University in California where she pursued another master's degree in Marriage and Family Therapy. On her way back to London she stopped in New York to visit family who encouraged her to get work experience in New York before returning to London. In New York she obtained employment, developed an interest in child welfare research which she began at Columbia University and was able to complete her doctoral degree in Social Work at Fordham University with a concentration in Children and Families. She also completed a doctoral degree in Christian Psychology.

The Corona Virus pandemic had a significant impact on Dr Valcourt and her desire to write this book because during this period she lost her father and brother-in-law, and her husband also lost several family members including his mother, uncle, aunt, sister and niece.

Printed in the United States
by Baker & Taylor Publisher Services